Singleness in a Marriage Shell

Theresa Shabani

Cover design by Spiffing Covers
Typeset and printed by Spiffing Covers
https://spiffingcovers.com/

About the Author

Theresa Shabani is a Keyworker with a lot of passion for children and has a strong spirituality background. She worked in the Department of Surveys and Mapping for 24 years in Gaborone, Botswana until she decided to change her career. She was born in Moroka Village in the North Eastern part of Botswana. She came to England in 2006 to do Business Studies but later decided to do her NVQ in Childcare Learning Development. During her spare time, she writes short stories for fun and Singleness in a marriage Shell is the first story to be published inspired by Women of Colour Study Bible.

Chapter 1

It was an extremely cold winter morning in October 1973. The temperatures were below zero. The inflexible bitter sky at night had turned unfriendly and ferocious with biting winds which could be heard hissing as they penetrated through the thin cracks of the window frames and the roof rattled with a vibrational resonance. Naniso had a disturbed sleep most of the night and just as she got into a deep sleep, she was woken up by the grating shrieks of her alarm. This was a perfect day for her to have stayed at home wrapped in her pyjamas with her fingers tightly playing around a thick mug of liquid offered with a layer of flavour complexity that highlighted the natural floral, caramel and roasted notes. She looked outside and saw that the white blanket had covered the ground and yet she had to face the rough journey to the bus stop with the solid crunch of her winter boots against the roadside.

The cold wind mercilessly whipped her face and chilled through to her bones. Oh! How it stung. She could feel her teeth chattering and the cold seeping into her gloves numbing her fingers until they ceased to bend properly. The pain numbed her feet through the boots and her skin felt raw. She tightened her hood around her face and the waiting was endless.

The bus ran behind schedule for the fog was so thick that it was difficult to see it until it was close. She had tears that fell from her eyes is if they would freeze. She painfully raised her hands to hail it. The bus ground to a halt slowly and carefully and a bulk of bodies with long faces, who dreaded to leave the warmth flooded out in the streets. She jumped in, her breath rose before her and puffs of moisture came from her lungs as she took a seat next to the window to avoid bumped by every person who walked by.

Chapter 2

Naniso was soft spoken with kind eyes. She had lips like a thread of scarlet, dropping as the honeycomb with milk and honey under her tongue. She was dark and lovely as if the sun had chosen her among thousands and looked upon her with sensible exposure. She grew up in Moroka village in Botswana with her parents and seven siblings. The sun always danced with joy in the mornings. It was beautifully warm, but in the evenings a gentle breeze brought a welcome coolness to the air. It seemed to be eternally summer. The woodland smelt of the summer rain. She woke up each morning at the sound of the cockerel, donkeys braying sometimes just for the hell of it and the rest of the livestock awaiting to be released into their freedom. Everyone knew almost everybody. Weddings, parties, ceremonies and funerals were attended without invitations… the true spirit of community.

She was the brightest of them all. She would walk several miles to school with her friends and most weekends during the ploughing season, she would journey miles and miles with her family, skipping like a calf along narrow roads with grass blowing in the wind and the sunlight penetrating through the trees tickling the landscape of her body and the flowers dancing happily in the sunshine. Ploughing was her family's real-life job. With strict rules and hard work, it was an organised physical activity which was rewarded generously at the end of the task when the ground gave its produce.

Now are the farmers born again
Quickened by sense and sight
Watching the sun baptise the grains
With a handful of streaming light

Okke Jagger

Naniso grew up in a very strict family not religious at that time. She grew up respecting her parents and everyone in her community regardless of age, though at times she played outside with her friends late on weekend evenings, copied their behaviours, mimicked people as they passed by, stirred up anger like the clouds which had gathered suspiciously and depressed the fading moon.

One man became very angry and took off in pursuit of her and her friends. Naniso ran very fast to save her skin, she kept running and out of the corner of her eye she could see him coming towards her. Her heart raised very loudly but she had to keep running. She tripped on a fence and fell like a bag of potatoes. She dragged herself up immediately and slumbered in silently before being noticed by her parents because she was bound for corporal punishment. Long time ago parents believed that you spared a rod and spoiled a child and every older person had the right to teach every child right or wrong for discipline was necessary for good upbringing.

Chapter 3

Naniso relocated to England when she was thirty- two years old for greener pastures, so she thought.

She realised things were different. The British ways and the weather far outweighed what she was used to. Everybody locked themselves indoors as if anticipating something scary following them. You never knew who your neighbours were except on some occasions the "neighbours from hell."

She walked down the stairs of New Hopes and was welcomed by an average lady. Her name was Rachel who might have been at that time in her mid-twenties, ordinary looking, not short, slim with tinted hair and hazel eyes fitly set. Her mouth and nose were mounted on the exact spots.

Cooking his face off with the aroma reaching her nose before her mouth was a middle aged, broad shouldered chef named Tom Adams with a friendly personality. He had tanned skin, heart-shaped face with brown, gentle eyes and coarse salt type of hair. His cheeks were protruding a little bit like dough with yeast taking a long time to rise. His clothing was elegant and polished. He sounded like freedom. Not just his words, but the way they tumbled gently from his lips.

"Please meet Tom and you will be working together." She said.

It was not love at first sight but having worked with him on several occasions, Naniso fell deeply in love with him. She wanted to know at least everything about him. She was fascinated by the way he walked, talked and smiled. She felt the closeness, energy and the chemistry that was different from any other man she had met before. She perfumed her bed with aloes and lavender with much seductive speech. She persuaded him with her smooth talk, gracious words like a honeycomb, sweetness to the soul.

"Falling in love again has never crossed my mind until I felt ants crawling all over my body." Naniso said.

"Your beauty is like the rising of the sun and you captivated and thrilled my heart with your smile." Said Tom. She compelled him and all at once he followed her like an ox to the slaughter.

Chapter 4

She gave up everything; her career as a Photogrammetrist in the Department of Surveys and Mapping, friends and family to be with the one she truly loved. She could not bear the separation, and the longing for him troubled her sleep. Even as she went about her daily tasks, her mind was on the love of her life, the man who swept her off her feet with the kind, gentle strengths and tender embraces.

She endured misunderstandings, temptations and pain to be together. Her love for him could not be quenched by many waters, neither be drowned by floods. She had no trouble spending lots of time with Tom listening to the continual dripping of water, sometimes hypnotised by the murmuring of the waves and the steady and peaceful palpitation pulse of the sea, hidden away from the buzz and whirr of the world and telling her loved one some amazing stories which he listened to with a lot of admiration for her and his favourite story was the one about Mabijo which was featured in one of her favourite magazine in a form of cartoons.

In the story Mabijo travelled to Mochudi to see his parents. He went to hitch- hike and yet had no money to pay for the journey. One driver who believed cash ruled everything around him gave him a lift.

"How much is the journey per head?" he asked.

"One hundred Pula." The driver said.

He jumped into the car, opened the window fully and stuck his head outside. The tears burst forth and spilled down his face like water from a well and the wind whooshed into his ears. The driver looked at him puzzled.

"why is your head outside the window?" asked the driver.

"Absorbing the smell of the wood-land," replied Mabijo.

When he arrived at his destination, he gave a hoot into his handkerchief and walked away.

"Excuse me Sir, you have forgotten to pay for your journey," the driver shouted.

"My head was outside the car," Mabijo replied.

Naniso and Tom spread their wings and the wind carried them miles and miles over the roaring seas, not all plain sailing but worth the price. She introduced him to her parents and wanted to ask them for her hand in marriage. A meeting with the older relatives was organised.

"Tom came here to ask for Naniso's hand in marriage."

said Alex, Naniso's Father.

One of the uncles who did not understand the English phrases stood up like a bullet, his voice grew louder like a storm in the distance whose approach cannot be prevented.

Why has he come to ask for a hand only…what about the rest of the body" he asked.

Chapter 5

Naniso had always dreamt and wanted a relationship that personifies love in its purest form-a monogamous relationship that had an abiding respect and replete and an assuming trust, friendship and tenderness. She wanted to become something that no one else could be to him. She wanted to be a trusted friend and a wife, a woman gifted with greatness, empowered to accomplish more especially God`s will, a crown of Glory and a special treasure.

She had imagined love and constant attention for a stronger relationship. She thought she had finally met a man who was polite, respectful, considerate and attentive to her needs and someone who could allow her to attend to his needs as well. She had wanted a relationship that is perfectly complemented by the gentle smoky flavoured aroma of love which supported one another, empowered one another, developed and embraced each other, talked side by side on the move somewhere slowly but assuredly. She was prepared to hold her family together by her wisdom instead of being destroyed by her foolishness (Proverbs 14:1).

Chapter 6

The flowers appeared on the earth; the time of the singing of the birds had come, and the voice of the turtledove is heard in our land; the fig tree ripens its figs and the vines are in blossom; they give forth fragrance.

The joints of her thighs were like jewels, her navel like a round goblet which wanted no liquor. Her belly was a heap of wheat set about the lilies.

-Songs of Solomon

Enduring much to be with the man she respected and submitted to, while she became unsettled with his mood swings caused by depression and alcohol addictions which were cleverly hidden in the beginning, sitting for weeks without moving, he groaned as if his flesh and body were consumed, days of unclean body and odour were an assault to her nose and eyes. She felt poured out like water, at times her heart melted like wax within her breasts and the troubles of her relationship were enlarged. Aloneness, bearing under many crosses of disappointments, she had made a pit, dug it out and was falling into the hole she had made.

How she had hated discipline and her heart

despised correction. Naniso had gone into adultery, swallowed before chewing, eaten the forbidden fruit and compromised her faith and relationship with God. She ignored all the signs and thought she could fix them by her own strengths because deeper in Tom`s heart was a donkey spirit. He could do anything for Naniso on days he felt like he could climb the mountain top, taking some of her responsibilities and burdens but at times with a reputation of stubbornness She had not listened to her spirit man but followed her head. She had felt unrest and found it hard to move on, scared of being judged. She felt like she had brought all kinds of strife and confusions to herself and reaped the consequences of the aftermath.

Chapter 7

The troubles of her heart were enlarged, she laid awake like a lonely sparrow on the house top. Her days passed like smoke and her strength dried up like a potsherd.

She was confronted by challenges and trials, she tried to remain slow to react even though she felt hurt, and sometimes found herself boiling within, she was willing to trust God enough to release her anger into his care. She tried to be a woman who acts with wisdom, gentleness, kindness than a woman who reacts quickly. She tried to be a woman who is secure in who she was and what she believed in. She tried to be a woman with the ability to survive the hardships of marriage and still maintain the strength of her body and mind. She tried to be a woman who build character with the capacity to respond in joy to the various situations of life. She tried to possess an exceptional yet subtle strength spiritually, emotionally and physically. When she went out, she would supress her feelings and put on a brave face.

A joyful heart is good medicine, but a crushed spirit dries the bones.

-Proverbs 17:22

She had forged the tradition of staying strong, to avoid living with the fear of losing her dignity. She did not seem to accept her powerlessness because she, after all, she is a strong woman. She had to guard her inner beauty because she did not want to walk around feeling like her flesh was decayed, her bone fallen into despair, disintegrated and dwindled.

Naniso had overlooked his quirks, blinded by love. Depression, alcohol addictions and the infidelity with her neighbour who also had the same issues... birds of a feather flock together. Naniso had finished work early on Wednesday afternoon and to her horror had found Tom sleeping in their bed with Annabel.

"Do you have any medical history I should know about?" She spat venom like a snake.

Naniso tried to open her mouth but no words came out. "Are you just going to stand there and not answer my question?"

Tom did not utter a word. He just sat there and avoided eye contact.

She felt a punch to the gut. Nothing worse had prepared her for the initial shock. She felt consumed by a sense of hurt and anger and felt her world crashing down. She was distraught, felt betrayed and disgusted. The marital dynamic had crumbled down. She could not accept that Tom`s addiction was a disease. She viewed it as a moral failure and lack of will power towards her.

She found herself not functioning anymore. Her marriage vows were openly broken and disregarded. She lost the zeal to submission, lost respect of her husband. At times she looked at him with so much hatred. She had known the fear that accompanied being abandoned as a married woman more especially intimately and affectionately. She felt like she had entered in a relationship with her eyes closed. She had revealed some of her secrets to Tom to trust her and to build a deeper connection with him and yet all his were intelligently hidden. She had expected more in their relationship: openness, happiness, trustworthy, maturity and satisfaction.

She was left feeling alone and disappointed and sometimes tempted to look elsewhere for a more meaningful relationship but at times felt that it was better the devil she knew than a wolf in sheep`s skin. She could not imagine dating again.

She started to live a life of no real communication. Tom disappeared into the unknown and she was restricted and suffocated by not having the ability of all whom she was. She had not followed the instructions from above again for the second time. He knew almost everything she did and yet she did not know most of what he did unless caught off guard. Naniso was not a good picker or maybe she was not a good fruit herself.

Chapter 8

Her first marriage was with Chikumbi from Malawi. He was young and handsome, he stood his head above the other men like a giraffe, with a dark complexion which seemed like dark chocolate had been brushed and worked well into his skin. He turned up two days before the wedding as if he came for a parade. She had paid the dowry herself to avoid embarrassment with her family. He only got in the wedding suit she bought and after the wedding, took most of their wedding gifts back to Malawi and left her alone for six years with just a ring in her finger and promises that turned to lies. What kind of love is it without actions, responsibilities and risks? She was left digging a well without water and filed for divorce. She found herself hopelessly trapped with no chance to escape the embarrassment and she avoided people for fear of being judged.

Pulling together with Tom was the hardest task she has ever experienced. This reminded her of years ago when farmers and even her family used cattle-mounted ploughs to cultivate their farmlands; two cows or two donkeys will be put together to pull a plough: this was known as an equal yoke but putting a cow and a donkey was unequal yoke since the two pulled in different directions with different strengths and mind set. She found herself faced with a stagnant marriage with different directions which did not meet at a cross- road. A marriage that withered like a garden without water.

Tom and Naniso slept together under the same roof but lived separate lives, went separate ways and done most things separately without working as a team which caused a lot of stagnation in their relationship. The marriage had silent treatment, unresolved deep intimate issues, resentment, addictive behaviours, emotional neglect, depression, secrecy and negativity.

Chapter 9

Her marriage was not fulfilling; she was lonely. She could not solve his problems, ask his opinions or learn about his new interests. There was no interdependence in each other`s lives. She always wondered why he did not want to connect with her, got involved with her, shared passions with her. She yearned day and night for his company, but her spouse resisted change. He was emotionally checked out and did not seem to care about her efforts to improve the situation. He was ashamed to extend his own efforts. She opened to him, forgave him as to go through the healing process but he had withdrawn himself and was gone. He felt embarrassed, avoided conversations and certain subjects which he would change for no apparent reason. The dogs were let down low to sleep.

She stopped pushing, urging, nudging, asking and begging and waited…but still no change. She tried to inspire him, show empathy, compassion and support, but these were dismissed with silence. She tried giving gifts which were never used or appreciated, tried favours, wrote letters to express her feelings, thoughts, hurts, expectations but not responded to. She tried touching, hugging, cuddling but felt like she was touching a frozen chicken.

She was denied all the opportunities of being made to feel like a woman and to enjoy the pleasures with Tom. The fire and the sweetness she had experienced in the beginning had vanished. She felt like she was a hedgehog, rolled into a ball, with sharp spikes that seemed to be extended to keep away all males and eventually most of her friends too. Cooking for him was loathed and despised.

Chapter 10

In the beginning, it was easy for her to give all she could to her spouse and enjoyed thinking of new ways to express how she felt through her giving. He had now lost interest in feeling her through those gifts whether it was his favourite author(book), or something he used to mention he liked... that did not make him glow and look at her with intense appreciation. She felt the world apart, both had their own schedules.

Abandonment has left Naniso feeling broken, and rejection had left her feeling unworthy. Her spouse was not prepared to break old habits of living a single life while still married to her. He did not sleep in the same bed with her, have meals with her, go on holidays with her, celebrate her birthday, or his birthday, let alone celebrate their wedding anniversary. He was very uncomfortable to be seen with her in public may be because of her ethnic roots. He was more comfortable doing what was familiar yet destructive than do what is unfamiliar but constructive.

The experience of loneliness became the reality at various times in her life. It was a frightening experience that left her with a sense of powerlessness. She became so tired of being tired that the thought of going on any longer was no longer appealing or meaningful. She felt like a wave of the sea driven and tossed by the wind and her beauty perished as if the sun had risen with its scorching heat and withered it like grass.

What a fool she was… to believe in the solace of change… for change robbed her of what she thought she knew. She used to be able to compose the melody of her life and paused the music and came back to it at her leisure…but the harmony was rearranged at every measure. She now failed to pick up the scattered notes of her marriage. She could not add warmth anymore to the beat of the icy heart.

Chapter 11

Hours, weeks, months, perhaps years passed when Naniso reached the point when she felt something need to change. She felt like everything in the world she revelled in seemed all wrong. It was almost hard to function anymore. She felt overwhelmed, disappointed by what is there. She lost control, hatred engulfed her like wildfire and she packed her suitcase and went to live with her friends to give each other space with the hope of both coming to their senses. She still loved Tom. You may say she was a dreamer… for she was in love and she strived to listen to the possible.

The space between them settled and fell as the snowfall. Naniso was a woman who could do many things in God`s creative world. She had the authority to be creative any day of the week. She was a woman who loved to watch the stars and the moon.

She was a free woman who was challenged, renewed, redirected until she allowed herself to be belittled, put down and betrayed. Naniso never thought she would find herself lonely in her marriage.

She thought she would be much happier than she was when she was single.

She nearly went into a deep depression. She was miles away from the rest of her immediate family. The depth and the despair that accompanied such feelings became fertile ground for thoughts of giving up, but her soul cried out to God in wordless prayers that emanated from holes so deeply hewn by despair that rescue sometimes felt incomprehensible. What God had said isn`t only alive and active, it`s sharper than any double- edged sword. His word cut through Naniso`s spirit and soul and through her joints and marrow until it discovered the thoughts of her heart. (Hebrews 4:12-14)

Despite Naniso being tossed about because of neglect, loneliness and her desires not met, she faced each day awaken to rediscover her true self, redeemed her positive self-image, and kept her heart guarded with beauty and the image of God which became the life force that gave her strength of character in the depth of life`s valleys and humility during the excruciating journey. She realised that she cannot keep chasing true love and happiness from Tom. She had to build values in herself.

She went back to becoming a woman of refinement and good manners. She stayed focussed and tried and tried again regardless of the circumstances and the conditions she found herself in. She continued to place one foot in front of the other. She persevered through the race. She kept her mind on things that are true, noble, just, pure, lovely and of good report to overcome the obstacles of loneliness and achieve her highest potential. She had the heart to forgive and the desire for what was at first-to a moment when things were good because she realised that in life you could be lonely when single, in a marriage or even in the crowd.

She saturated her consciousness with the word of God until it penetrated and filled the hollow places of her soul. Coping became the language of transition. She shook off the trash and the dust the relationship dished. She became the woman who had the capacity to respond with joy to the various situations of life even in the middle of a troubled world where being gracious was difficult.

To stay in her marriage, Naniso kept her vows of being in a marriage for better or for worse. She tried to do what was right and kept her conscience clear. She spent years trying to win back his love. She thought she had finally found someone she could build a family with. She yearned each day to be his confidante, encourager, helper and inward strength. his worth, she literally wanted to be part of him but she found herself waiting as if she was waiting for a medical exam, scared to what the results would be, or encountered turbulences as if she was in an aeroplane and sometimes sad as if she has been to a funeral. But, despite all that she lived with hope and continued to carry sunshine in her heart believing and trusting God that it was a season which shall pass in due time.

God changed her character and gave her peace that surpassed human understanding. Peace that flowed like a river.

She tried to improve her communication skills-which is the most important task in creating a successful marriage, maintained her emotions and insecurities with meditations, made adjustments and at times compromised as she learnt to live with him year after year, tried to create a "we" which was reconstructing a shared meaning in her relationship based on friendship, common ground, similar goals, worked together and commitment with respect, attractiveness, worth learning about and celebrating, but her spouse remained a brick wall that could not be cracked for her to slide in. He refused silently and sometimes with a lot of anger and constantly played mind games to make her feel guilty.

At times Naniso found herself so exhausted by putting a lot of effort towards improving and making her marriage work because her spouse showed no respect and love for her. She tried to provide the right environment in which he can shine and therefore be a better partner to love her openly, but all was disregarded by silence, secrecy and privacy. He did not think there was anything wrong. He was going about doing whatever he wanted without any consideration of how she felt.

She came to realise that she was married to a confirmed bachelor, someone who is used to living alone, going and coming back as he pleases, without answering to anyone, sleeping alone, eating alone and at times treating her like she did not exist.

Chapter 12

A lot happened between Naniso and Tom that sometimes weighed on her. The longer she "held them in," the heavier the burden became. She could not get deeper into his heart to see what was bothering him or what his frustrations were. She desperately wanted to know and draw all that he cannot let go of and help him finally heal and get his life back, but all she felt was like knocking on a door of an empty house. How she felt the void of love she could give to Tom, how she longed to laugh and giggle but only silence and the pain of solitude screamed at her and failure to her un-wavered nerve took her vast appetite for sacrifice.

Sometimes Naniso wished she had wings like an eagle and fly away and simply escape the emptiness, but instead she decided to enjoy her own company. She stopped carrying the burden and handed over it to God in prayer. She would prepare herself some candle lit dinner and stood in front of the mirror, danced her frustrations away, celebrated herself for no one celebrated her and she felt live again with energy, excitement and enthusiasm.

Chapter 13

Naniso did not want to be determined by someone else`s actions but instead be guided by the wisdom of God. She became a woman who survived the hardships of marriage and still maintained her character with the capacity and responded with joy to the various situations in her life. She became a woman who acted with wisdom and gentleness. She became a woman who is secure on who she was and what she believed in.

She bounced back from life`s disappointments that defined how successful she could be. She got back on the right course. The creator of the universe recalculated her purpose to get her back on the right path.

Regardless of how many times she was knocked down, beaten, God always cared for her and His love which served as the ultimate, true example of a pure love sustained her and gave her the strength to face each day with a positive mind; love that is unconditional, love that bears all things, hopes all things and endures all things.(1 corinthians 13:7). She dwelt in the presence of God for security, well-being and protection and wisdom that comes down from above which is first pure, then peaceable, gentle, open to reason, full of mercy and good fruits, impartial and sincere. And a harvest of righteousness is sown in peace by those who make peace. She made peace with herself and changed her attitude. She learnt to forgive herself to have the power to move out of the past and into the present which gave her control over her life.

God became a secure place for her to stand in times of life`s disappointments, fears and doubts and He turned her gloom into light. He restored her and made her strong, firm and steadfast. Strength and dignity became her clothing. Somewhere between her despair and self-pity, she developed a thick skin, a steady mind, boldness, courage and a right head on her shoulders and took on the world. She became anything she wanted to be. She believed in herself. She stepped out of her comfort zone and build the life she wanted for herself. Armed with God`s promises, she ran the race to reach the goal with a positive attitude and held on to the truth that catapulted her to the mountain top where she gazed at a world full of possibilities.

Printed in Great Britain
by Amazon